Praise for HOPE: A Practical Guide to Praying for Healing by Rebecca Ribnick

I have had the great privilege of seeing this wonderful book first lived out in and through Rebecca's life. Her own incredible personal healing was the spark that ignited this intense fire and desire to help encourage the body of Christ to better understand and minister divine healing. I have personally been inspired by watching Rebecca practice what she shares throughout this book. She has seen many, many people healed in this wonderful journey and I believe *HOPE: A Practical Guide to Praying for Healing* will be a game changer for all who read it.

JASON CHIN
Founder of Love Says Go Ministries (Basel, Switzerland)
Author of *Love Says Go*

The question of "Does God still heal today?" has plagued many of us as believers. In her book, *HOPE,* Rebecca comes alongside us like a world-class coach with practical tools grounded in biblical truth to answer that question and reorient our thinking about healing. Rebecca and *HOPE* give us permission to be ourselves and to be on our own journey. By the end of the book, you will feel like a runner with your feet planted at your starting block, ready to begin the great race that God has before you. I highly recommend this resource as a practical, powerful, and potential igniting tool.

KRISTEN D'ARPA
Founder of i Go Glocal and Kristen D'Arpa Ministries
Author of *Kingdom Culture School of Ministry* curriculum

HOPE: A Practical Guide to Healing is not a book—but an invitation. This book is for those who want more of God, are not satisfied with one more sermon, book, or lecture on propositional truth or are fed up with spiritual life meetings promising five ways, guaranteed or money back, to revive one's soul. Additionally, this book is for those who see the power of God to heal, so prevalent in the Gospels and book of Acts, but wonder why we see little today. This is an honest book and has the feel of a friendly conversation with Ribnick in Starbucks. Be careful: As you again think of God's love and the power of the kingdom of God amongst us, perhaps you, like Rebecca, will be forever changed.

DR. ROBERT DUFFETT
Former president of Eastern University (Philadelphia, Pennsylvania)

ISBN-13: 978-1-7328934-3-6

Edited by Lauren Stinton
Cover Design & Layout by Jonathan McGraw

Printed in the United States of America

Visit the author's website at: rebeccaribnick.com

Speaking
SPIRIT *to* SPIRIT

A BIBLICAL LOOK AT PRAYING IN TONGUES

REBECCA RIBNICK

WAIT. WHAT JUST HAPPENED?

"Dude, I'm kind of freaked out," I tell my mentor as soon as we reach the room we're sharing.

"Yeah, this is a strange life moment!" she says.

We break out in nervous laughter. You know, the kind that prevents you from crying.

We are entirely off the grid in a little village on a remote Southeast Asian island. As is customary in these villages where there are no hotels, we stay in the home of the village leader, who in this case happens to be a regionally renowned witch doctor. I don't have words to describe everything I've experienced or seen with my own eyes in this village. It is unsettling. And really weird.

"I mean, I'm freaked out," I repeat when our laughter subsides.

"Yeah, this is pretty crazy," she agrees. "If it's okay with you, I'm going to pray in tongues for a minute."

I have a few reservations about it—I have never heard anyone pray in tongues—but I trust my friend and we need divine help.

As she begins to pray softly, I analyze what I hear; the cadence and unique sounds seem like a language, albeit one I do not recognize. More than that, I notice how I *feel*. The anxiety and fear lift as she prays. When she stops, I am at peace for the first time since we arrived.

Contrary to all of the negatives I've heard about tongues, I am a little jealous. I wish I could do that—draw on the Spirit of God that way and crush fear. But I brush the thought away with platitudes: "I don't have that gift," and "If God wanted me to have it, he'd give it to me."

WHERE IT BEGINS

Regardless of your exposure to speaking in tongues, I think we can all agree that it is a polarizing subject. Odds are that you and I began in a similar place. No, not a witch doctor's house (I'm guessing that is unique to my story), but with an understanding more often inferred from the opinions of those around us than taught from a biblical perspective. Simply put, there is little teaching and a lot of confusion surrounding this topic.

The devil is not omnipotent. His power is limited. It is simply not worth his effort to sow confusion, discord, and division over something of little value. Somewhat counterintuitively, the mess surrounding tongues actually signals the presence of something highly valuable for us to discover.

What follows is an introduction to praying in tongues as a personal prayer language (also called *speaking in tongues, praying in the Spirit,* or simply *tongues).*

We will look at the benefits of praying in tongues, as well as some of the reasons people hesitate to pray this way; address a few common concerns; and conclude with a practical how-to guide—so we can start to see this incredible grace operating in our lives in a healthy, biblically ordained way.

MY STORY

There is a reason Jeep advertisements feature the vehicle traversing rugged terrain. Seeing something operating in its designed purpose helps us picture what it could look like in our lives. That night in the witch doctor's house was my first in-person encounter with praying in tongues, and it caught my attention. I saw firsthand that speaking in tongues is real, powerful, and packs a big punch. I pictured what it could look like in my life and I wanted it. Like, I *really* wanted it.

Instead of that moment springboarding an energetic pursuit of tongues, my denominational presupposition that I passively wait for whatever God might want to give me shut me down. I went to bed with peace regarding the demonic activity . . . and also guilt over my desire to speak in tongues.

Fast forward six months. I am back stateside and am both deeply hungry for more of God and deeply frustrated because I don't know how to satisfy that hunger. I read the Bible longer, pray harder, and volunteer more hours, but to no avail. I reach out to my mentor in Southeast Asia for suggestions. This is how I find myself at the gym listening to a recorded sermon from a missionary named Heidi Baker.

This is my first time hearing Heidi preach. Her intimacy with God makes me uncomfortable, but she also speaks with an authority that compels me to listen. I cannot turn the sermon off. Heidi has a unique preaching style in which she preaches in English but interjects Portuguese. I understand basic Portuguese so I can follow a lot of what she says, but there are some strange words I don't recognize.

And then it hits me—the words I do not recognize are not Portuguese but from her own prayer language. Heidi is speaking in tongues!

When the shock wears off, I try to assign meaning to these strange words the same way I do her Portuguese. *Okay*, I think, *that means "Praise Jesus" in Portuguese, so when she speaks the other language right after it, it probably means the same thing.*

I realize what I'm doing and instantly feel silly. *Becca!* I chide myself. *No one learns tongues the same way they learn Portuguese.*

That's not how it works.

A voice interrupts my self-criticism. It is as clear as someone speaking audibly: "Who told you that?"

My heart leaps inside me. I jump off the treadmill, grab my bag, and head home. I do not understand what is happening, but I know that *I know* God just spoke to me.

Back at my house, I go straight to my bedroom. My mind is reeling, yet excitement bubbles inside me. In my sweaty gym clothes, I kneel beside my bed and, with no other thoughts or prayers, I open my mouth and try to speak.

WHAT IS TONGUES?

I vividly remember certain things from that day—like exactly where I was (to the left of the bed, near the bookcase), how the basement floor felt cold on my knees, and that something deep within me felt invigorated and refreshed. I also remember a weighty, tangible peace that reminded me of a child sleeping on her mother's lap.

However, other aspects are fuzzy. I don't remember the actual sounds that came out of my mouth, but I know they were far from the easy fluency with which I pray in tongues now. Even though I heard myself speaking a language I did not understand or recognize, I was still a little skeptical of the whole thing. And honestly, I felt foolish.

For me, learning what the Bible says about tongues helped remove doubt, fear, and misunderstanding surrounding the subject. According to the simple definition presented in Scripture, speaking in tongues is a manifestation of the Holy Spirit for personal encouragement, growth, and maturation in the nature and character of Christ. There are other aspects as well, but we will specifically look at tongues as a personal prayer language, which the apostle Paul wrote about in 1 Corinthians 14:2–4.

To really understand how speaking in tongues "works," we need to pause and remember that we were made in the image of our triune God and that we are also triune in nature. First Thessalonians 5:23 tells us that we are spirit, soul, and body. Our spirit is *already* seated in heavenly places with every spiritual blessing in Christ (Eph. 1:3; 2:6). The soul is our emotions, will, and mind, while the body is what we experience through our five senses.

The spirit needs to steer the ship of our lives. Living with the spirit in charge gives us access to heaven's unlimited resources, including divine wisdom and heavenly perspective. Conversely, when the soul drives our lives, we are limited to what our human emotions, willpower, and mind understand. Living with our body in charge empowers the physical world to become more significant to us than the eternal realm of God's kingdom. The end result is the same whether it is our soul or our body that usurps our spirit's leadership: living from our perspective and wisdom instead of God's. The spirit, soul, and body are all wonderful and important, but there is an intended divine order within them that governs how we live.

Praying in tongues is a direct line from our spirit to God. Tongues bypasses our soul and is therefore not limited to what we understand or feel. It makes little sense to our minds, but our reason and logic are often offended in a kingdom where we go low to go high and where we lose our life to find it. Praying in tongues cuts through all of the noise, miscommunication, and lack of understanding that come from this world, and it links us directly to our eternal home.

WHY YOU WANT THIS (THE BENEFITS)

Love is the operating system of heaven. Praying in tongues is like running a system cleanup on our devices, getting rid of bugs and upgrading the OS. The Bible calls this kind of housecleaning and building up *edification*. Paul wrote, "Anyone who speaks in a tongue edifies themselves" (1 Cor. 14:4). Praying in tongues builds up our spirit (and in turn, our soul and body) as we declare the truths of God over ourselves and our circumstances. Tongues strengthens our spirit the same way weight training and protein shakes build our muscles.

Here is a quick look at some of the benefits of praying in tongues.

Praying with Heaven

Too many times to count, I have found myself in a place or frame of mind where the last thing I want to do is pray—and that is a perfect time to pray in tongues. God is never discouraged or disappointed about anything I face, and when I pray in tongues, my spirit gets his perspective. I find my mood quickly shifts, and whatever was bothering me gets put in its proper place even before my mind understands.

In part, this divine exchange occurs because I am no longer praying by myself. The Bible says that God prays for us (Rom. 8:26; Heb. 7:25). When we pray in tongues, we add an earthly amen to the heavenly prayers that Jesus and the Holy Spirit are already praying on our behalf. Our prayers become the third strand in a cord of three that can hold the weight of all the problems, fears, cares, and concerns we could ever face.

Expressing the Inexpressible

My appreciation for art has grown tremendously over the years. I used to not "get it," but slowly I began to see that art has the potential to express things otherwise inexpressible. Art can capture emotion, pain, process, and beauty in a way our words struggle to express. It is why certain paintings speak to us. Art transcends the limits of our verbal communication and has the potential to lift us from the terrestrial to the celestial.

So, too, praying in tongues takes us above and beyond what we can wrap our words around. It frees us to praise, release our pain, and express love in a place deeper and higher than our known vocabulary can reach.

Praying in tongues also allows us to pray when we have absolutely no idea *what* to pray. There are plenty of times I do not know what to pray, or I struggle praying because the subject is too painful. Praying in tongues frees me to pray in spite of my pained emotions or lack of understanding. It carries my prayers above my own soulish limitations and connects me to the love, joy, and peace of heaven, all while giving God access to every part of me, so he can touch those parts with his healing and sanctifying grace.

Deep Mysteries and Praise

It gets even better. The Bible tells us that the Holy Spirit searches the deep things of God (1 Cor. 2:10). When we pray in tongues, our spirit speaks these mysteries aloud and praises God (1 Cor. 14:2; Acts 10:46). So in addition to praying exactly what Jesus and the Holy Spirit are praying for us, we also speak out the mysteries of God and glorify him.

Our words are powerful. We were made in the image of Creator God who spoke everything into being. Proverbs tells us that our words contain life and death (18:21). My mind literally cannot grasp the depth of God's goodness, the breadth of his love, nor take in his astounding beauty. Praying in tongues allows me to declare the wonders of who he is into this world even before my mind grasps the truth. No wonder Paul said he prayed in tongues all the time and encouraged us to do likewise (1 Cor. 14:5, 18).

Miracles

From a violent storm that calmed before my eyes to deaf ears that opened, from miraculously avoiding an accident to connecting with just the right person who helped solve a troubling problem, time and again I have seen incredible miracles when I pray in tongues—too many to list here. Testimonies inspire our hearts to dream about what God will do in and through us, and they reveal his unchanging nature. "The testimony of Jesus is the spirit of prophecy" (Rev. 19:10 NASB). As we recount testimonies of what God has done, our expectation for that aspect of God's nature to be demonstrated in *our* lives grows. The same God who works miracles when I pray in tongues will work miracles when you pray in tongues.

The more testimonies I hear about what happens when we pray in tongues, the more expectant I become for what God will do in my life.[1]

---

1. If you want to be ridiculously inspired to pray in tongues, check out *Chasing the Dragon* by English missionary Jackie Pullinger. Jackie worked among some of the most ruthless gangs in the world in the walled city of Hong Kong. Her classic biography is jam-packed with testimony after testimony of what happens when we pray in tongues. She even saw people freed from heroin addictions without any withdrawal symptoms.

The Many Benefits of Speaking in Tongues

In summary, here are a few things that happen as a result of praying in tongues:

1. We pray directly to God from our spirit in perfect agreement with his will for any situation.
2. Praying in tongues enables us to access a deeper level of prayer and worship than our known languages allow.
3. As we pray in tongues, we declare the mysteries of God.
4. Miracles abound as we access this divine grace.

In addition to those benefits, speaking in tongues also builds us up to believe, think, and behave more like Jesus.

SO WHAT'S THE HOLDUP?

Though I spent my childhood in Sunday school and youth group, attended a Christian university, and participated in countless Bible studies, I was in my mid-twenties before I ever heard a teaching on praying in tongues—and it was full of personal opinions with a strong denominational (instead of scriptural) bent. The absence of solid, biblical teaching is perhaps the greatest hindrance to seeing this powerful tool in the hands of every believer. A secondary issue is the abuse and misuses that some have experienced around tongues. (These tend to be referenced offhandedly instead of intentionally addressed.)

In this section, let's take a look at some of the common assumptions that can keep us from praying in tongues.

"I Don't Have the Gift"

"I don't have the gift" and "God might not want it for me" effectively shut down my pursuit of praying in tongues moments after I experienced the Holy Spirit's power displayed at the witch doctor's house. With no biblical teaching on the gifts of the Spirit in general, let alone tongues, I could not combat those lies with truth. Only later did I learn that praying in tongues is not a special gift limited to a select few. It is available to *every believer.*

Paul's teaching about the gifts of the Holy Spirit is primarily found in 1 Corinthians 12. The chapter starts, "Now concerning spiritual *gifts,* brothers *and sisters,* I do not want you to be unaware" (v. 1 NASB). If you are using a study Bible, you will see the word *gifts* italicized. An italicized word is added by the translator for clarity and isn't found in the original language. In this instance, it creates confusion. Lost in translation is the fact that there is only *one* gift—the Holy Spirit himself. The list in 1 Corinthians 12 doesn't reference gifts we may or may not receive, but it's a description of the gift we all receive—the Holy Spirit, who manifests through believers in different ways for God's glory and our benefit.

All of us come to faith in Jesus through the Holy Spirit's work. The Bible says that he lives within us and serves as a seal for our heart, an engagement ring to all of God's promises (John 14:17; 2 Cor. 1:22). Discussions about the Holy Spirit and baptisms can quickly turn into divisive doctrinal issues, so instead of debating, let's just take a quick look at the early Christians' encounters with the Holy Spirit:

- Jesus breathes on his disciples in John 20:22 and says, "Receive the Holy Spirit."
- Jesus tells the same disciples he breathed on to wait in Jerusalem until they receive the Holy Spirit (Luke 24:49; Acts 1:8).

- The Holy Spirit fills the disciples (Acts 2:4).
- The same people filled with the Holy Spirit in Acts 2 are filled with the Holy Spirit again in Acts 4 (vv. 23–31).

Clearly, receiving a filling, a fresh touch, or whatever language we wrap around an encounter with the Holy Spirit is not meant to be a one-time experience. Instead of limiting how much of the Holy Spirit we can have, Scripture sets a great example for us to continually ask for—and expect—more of the Holy Spirit in our lives. How much of the Holy Spirit can we have? I am not sure, but until we look just like Jesus, there is room for more.

More often than not, God gives things to us in seed form, sowing into the soil of our lives small beginnings that grow as we steward them. The more I value the Holy Spirit's fellowship and work in me, the more of him I want in my life and, in turn, the more God fills me with himself. All I need to do is ask (see Luke 11:11–13).

The idea that we might not have "the gift of tongues" is at best a misunderstanding of what is available to us and at worst an intentional avoidance of the discomfort that often comes from pursuing something outside a denominational teaching. Simply put, belief in Jesus gives us access to the greatest resource heaven has for us—the Holy Spirit—and through him we are enabled and empowered to pray in tongues.

"If God Wants Me to Have Tongues, He Will Give It to Me"

Picture this: You are a sprinter in the finals of the biggest track meet of the season. All day long you cheer on your teammates as you wait for your event to be called. You nibble on protein bars and bananas; you attempt to stay relaxed and not think about the months of training it took to get here.

Finally it is time for your race. You head down to the starting line and check that your blocks are just so. You shake out your legs and remove your warmups. The noise of the crowd disappears and the world around you moves in slow motion as the announcer calls you to your mark. Your razor-like focus dials all the way in as you put your feet in the starting blocks. You take a deep breath before settling down on one knee. At last you hear the word you are waiting for: "Set," the announcer calls. Pushing your weight up and back, your legs coil like springs as you wait for the starter's gun.

But the gun never sounds.

Left in the starting blocks in the set position is how I felt for many years of my Christian walk as I continually focused on the message of salvation without moving on to the message of kingdom transformation. God calls us to bring transformation to the earth until it looks like heaven (Matt. 6:10). Each of us is divinely assigned a race to run that pours transformation through our lives into the world around us (Eph. 2:10). Salvation is the entry to our race; Bible reading, spiritual disciplines, and church attendance can train us for it—but these things are not the race itself. The Holy Spirit and his manifestations empower and equip us to run the race marked out for us.

Paul fully understood our assignment and how much we need the Holy Spirit's manifestations if we want to accomplish it. When he wrote, "Earnestly desire spiritual *gifts*" (1 Cor. 14:1, NASB), he was not offering a friendly suggestion. *Zēloō* is the Greek word for "desire," and it means "to burn with zeal," "to strive after," and "to exert one's self for."[2] *Zēloō* is a command. When it comes to pursuing tongues and the manifestation of the Spirit in our lives, Paul did not

---

2. James Strong, *The New Strong's Exhaustive Concordance of the Bible,* expanded ed. (Nashville: Thomas Nelson, 2010), word number 2206.

leave us stranded on the starting blocks; instead, he directed us to the finish line of an earth that looks like heaven—and fired the gun.

"I Feel Foolish"

Let's head back to Southeast Asia for a hot minute (pun intended).

At this point, I've been in the country for a couple of months, and I'm at a Pizza Hut celebrating a friend's birthday. (I swear, Pizza Hut is the place to go for celebrations in this country.) My roommate, who speaks the local language, tells me she is not returning directly home and asks if I can find my way on my own. I self-consciously assure her I can, but truthfully I can't. I have no idea how to get home, nor do I speak the language well enough to ask for help, and I am too embarrassed to admit it. Compounding my shame, one by one, my local friends ask if I need help getting home, and inexplicably I say no to each one of them. My embarrassment over not understanding the language cuts me off from much-needed help and nearly strands me at a Pizza Hut.[3]

For many of us, one of the highest hurdles to praying in tongues is the same thing that trips us up when learning a language: We feel foolish. Pride stands in the way of the humility necessary to step out in faith. Fortunately, we do not need to perfectly understand how praying in tongues works to experience its benefits.

Earlier we discussed that praying in tongues comes from our spirit, not our mind (soul). There are interesting studies that confirm this. *The New York Times* even wrote an article about this very topic, stating:

Researchers at the University of Pennsylvania took brain images of five women while they spoke in tongues and found that their frontal lobes—the thinking, willful part of the brain through

---

3. Clearly, I made it home. A friend very kindly recognized my predicament, told me he "needed" to swing by my house, and offered to give me a ride. I am still grateful for his kindness.

which people control what they do—were relatively quiet, as were the language centers. The regions involved in maintaining self-consciousness were active.[4]

I love how this research validates what we already know, namely that the mind does not fully grasp what happens spirit-to-Spirit.

Scripture governs something's role in my life, not how well I understand the topic. For instance, I don't understand how the blood of Jesus covers all of my sins—past, present, and future—yet I do not let my lack of comprehension of the power of his blood limit my response. In the same way, my incomplete comprehension of tongues does not limit my use of this incredible grace. Jesus perfectly modeled humility for us (see Phil. 2:1–10), and in my choice to be like him, I am willing to humbly embrace what I cannot comprehend for the sake of his kingdom.

"I Don't Feel Anything"

The first time I experienced the power of praying in tongues, I felt peace as a byproduct of my friend's prayers. The next time I encountered it, the night I began speaking in tongues myself, I again felt peace. For me, peace often accompanies times of praying in tongues—but not always. There are plenty of times I pray in tongues without feeling anything at all. The idea that we must *feel something,* be it ecstatic euphoria or deep-seated stillness, is a misconception. As with any spiritual discipline or relationship, feeling something is not proof of its power; the actual proof of tongues' power is the evidence of the Holy Spirit's work in us. Instead of asking what I feel, I like to ask myself if I am believing, thinking, and behaving more like Jesus.

---

4. Benedict Carey, "A Neuroscientific Look at Speaking in Tongues," *New York Times,* November 7, 2006, https://www.nytimes.com/2006/11/07/health/07brain.html.

"I Might Be Deceived"

Another common misconception I run into concerning praying in tongues is a fear that the devil is deceiving us. This misconception carries two distinct suggestions:

1. That praying in tongues is merely pointless babbling (not true communication with God) or
2. That praying in tongues is actually the demonic speaking through us instead of the Holy Spirit.

Fortunately for us, the Bible gives us clear guidelines to help us recognize when the Holy Spirit is leading us. These guidelines are commonly called *the fruit of the Spirit* (see Gal. 5:22–23). The demonic does not make us feel more peaceful, lead us to love better, or encourage us to live with greater gentleness or patience, and it certainly does not fan the flame of our love for Jesus. The Holy Spirit does. We can know with full confidence that the Holy Spirit is praying with and through us when we pray in tongues as we examine the fruit of our prayer life to see if it matches the fruit of the Holy Spirit.

We can also reassure ourselves as we read Paul's directive to "pray in the Spirit on all occasions" (Eph. 6:18). Regular Bible study, spiritual disciplines, and healthy Christian community are further safeguards against deception and are vital to our faith walk.

The Holy Spirit is the Spirit of truth sent to guide us into all truth (John 16:13). I am more convinced of the Holy Spirit's ability to lead me into truth than I am of the devil's ability to deceive me. If I ever feel afraid to step beyond my comfort zone and walk by faith instead of what I understand, I like to remind myself that the Holy Spirit wants me to look more like Jesus and that he will never deceive me. When fear creeps up on us, we can pause, turn our hearts and minds to God, and ask him to lead us in truth. Then we simply follow his peace—a peace we cannot talk ourselves into and the enemy cannot fake.

Generally speaking, surrendering cognitive understanding and a sense of control in favor of walking by faith is scary. Surrender requires us to actively trust God in ways we don't have to when we feel in control. Surrender is contrary to the world's operating system. But surrendering to the Holy Spirit beyond what we understand is a hallmark of the Christian life: "For those who are led by the Spirit of God are the children of God" (Rom. 8:14).

"I'm Just Not Sure"

Much hesitancy about tongues is due to misuses and abuses that occurred because of a lack of biblical teaching. I grew up hearing that the only people who spoke in tongues were fraudulent TV evangelists or people who were trying to prove *they* had the Holy Spirit but others didn't. Sadly, all of the negative speculation surrounding praying in tongues dictated my course of action more than Scripture did.

It is worth reiterating that the devil intentionally sows confusion and misinformation around those things that are of great benefit to the body of Christ. Instead of allowing someone's misuse to keep us from pursuing praying in tongues, we can let the confusion surrounding tongues act as the *X* on a map pointing out where the treasure lies.

What a humbling thought, that God entrusts something as powerful as praying in tongues to his children, knowing we will make mistakes with it. Is it possible for someone to *fake* speaking in tongues? Yes. Is it possible to use tongues in a manner contrary to Paul's directive? Sure. But should those possibilities keep us from speaking in tongues? Paul answered that one for us: "Do not forbid speaking in tongues" (1 Cor. 14:39). Biblical directives, not someone's mistake or error, need to set our course.

"I Need an Interpreter If I'm Going to Speak in Tongues"

Speaking in tongues is a lot like riding in an elevator; it moves in two directions: up and down. When tongues are "moving down" (i.e., God is speaking to others through us), we interpret the message so all may benefit. Paul wrote that a top-down message from God requires translation (1 Cor. 14:26–28). However, when tongues are moving in the opposite direction (we are praying to God), there is no need for interpretation because God understands us perfectly. The setting does not determine the need for translation; the intended recipient does. Simply put, tongues as a personal prayer language, even in a corporate setting, needs no interpretation.

That said, my belief that praying in tongues is permissible according to biblical guidelines is secondary to whether or not my use of tongues is beneficial to everyone present. There are some settings where praying aloud in tongues may upset, offend, or dishonor other believers. In this setting, I will either pray under my breath or wait until I am alone out of respect for my brothers and sisters in Christ. As Paul wrote, "Take care that this freedom of yours does not somehow become a stumbling block" to others (1 Cor. 8:9 NASB). Whatever we do, whether praying in tongues or not, our green light is love and our heart posture is humility.

Living Outside Your Comfort Zone

The first time I went skydiving, an instructor briefly explained what to expect, strapped me into my harness, and got me in the plane all within ten minutes of my arrival at the airfield. While I was grateful that I didn't have time to think about what I was do-ing, you'd better believe I double-checked that the parachute was on correctly, and I tugged at my harness straps to make sure they were tight.

While not all of us feel like jumping from a plane, we are all called to live beyond our comfort zones. We get to boldly declare our belief in what Scripture says and cling to it even when it carries us beyond what we understand or what our experiences suggest. In other words, "we live by faith, not by sight" (2 Cor. 5:7). Living by faith takes us far beyond what we currently think is possible—but it doesn't mean we don't check with our instructor about the parachute or cinch our harness straps a little tighter.

In the context of praying in tongues, we "check with our instruc-tor" by being honest and sharing with God about our concerns or any holdups we experience as we pursue this beautiful manifesta-tion of the Holy Spirit. Likewise, we double-check our harness by making sure that Scripture determines our actions, not inadequate or absent teaching or our feelings of foolishness or offense.

By all means, check with the Great Instructor and tug on the safe-ty harness that is Scripture, but don't stay seated in the plane when you were born to fly.

HOW TO START

Praying in tongues edifies us, adds an earthly amen to heavenly prayers, and glorifies King Jesus. We know speaking in tongues is available to us all and is a powerful tool in building the kingdom of God. And we know that Paul commanded we pursue praying in tongues.

So there's just one final question left to answer: How do we do it?

Ask

Jesus said, "Ask and it will be given to you; seek and you will find; knock and the door will be opened to you" (Matt. 7:7). Similarly, the apostle James admonished that we have not because we ask not (Jas. 4:2). A child does not feel guilty or selfish about asking her parent for a drink of water when she's thirsty. So, too, we don't need to hold back from asking God for the things that lead us into Christlikeness.

The first step to activating a lifestyle of praying in tongues is simple: Ask God for the ability to do so.

Believe

The Bible says, "And whatever you ask in prayer, believing, you will receive it all" (Matt. 21:22 NASB; see also Mark 11:24). In the same way that eternal salvation requires only that we believe in Jesus, speaking in tongues is as simple as asking God for this beautiful grace in our lives and then believing he's given it to us.

Step two flows easily from step one: Ask and then believe you received.

Try

I used to think that the Holy Spirit's manifestations would just appear out of the blue fully developed in my life. Surely it would be like Mozart sitting at a piano and playing a masterpiece without practice or the need for instruction. While there may be a Mozart or two out there, the Holy Spirit's work in our lives usually begins as a tiny seed that grows as we steward it.

Faith in the kingdom of God is spelled R-I-S-K. Our pursuit of God requires action. Or as James wrote, faith without works is dead

(Jas. 2:17). The last step toward a lifestyle of praying in tongues is the one most often overlooked: Try.

For those of us who read the word *try* and immediately think, *How do I try?* here are a few tips:

- Don't overthink it.
- Don't worry about sounding silly or feeling foolish.
- Open your mouth and say whatever comes to you. If it's one syllable, repeat that syllable. Like building a muscle, as you use what you have, more will come.[5]

I began speaking in tongues the night I listened to Heidi Baker. I stumbled my way forward by repeating a couple of syllables. That was it. It was in no way comparable to the vocabulary, nuances, and ease with which I pray in tongues now. As I stewarded the awkward-sounding syllables that stumbled out of my mouth, they grew into the prayer language that now comes so naturally.

Finally, don't compare yourself to anyone else. The fastest way we can shut down growth and close ourselves off from heavenly grace is comparison. What God is doing in you is not the same thing that he is doing in me.

Activating a lifestyle of praying in tongues really is this simple: Ask. Believe. Try.

---

5. While it may *seem* like you're saying only one syllable, it's possible more is happening. Some of us have trouble distinguishing words and phrases in tonal languages such as Mandarin or Thai; there might be more happening than our ears can catch. God does things like that sometimes.

PARTING THOUGHTS

Rarely in life does a truly small upfront risk carry so much potential for a huge return. Honestly, the worst-case scenario when pursuing praying in tongues is that we feel foolish. That's as bad as it gets.

But let's look at the flip side—what happens if we try and are successful? The best-case scenario is that we communicate directly to God, pray in alignment with heaven, build ourselves up, glorify Jesus in a new and deep way, and see great power come into our lives. The reward outweighs the risk. We have nothing to lose.

Don't just take my word that praying in tongues will positively and powerfully impact your life, but put it to the test. Set a timer and pray in tongues for five minutes every day for a week. At the end of the week, ask yourself if you are experiencing more fruit of the Holy Spirit and if you look more like Jesus. (Remember, peace or the ability to forgive someone is as supernatural as multiplying food and walking on water.) If it's too soon to tell, do it for one more week. If you look more like Jesus and if there is more love, joy, peace, patience, kindness, goodness, gentleness, or self-control around you, you have your answer.

PRAY WITH ME

The benefit in my life from praying in tongues leads me to say exactly what Paul said: I wish we all prayed in tongues. And fortunately, due to God's great kindness and his desire for us to live like Jesus, this gift is available to us all. Ask. Believe. Try.

Father, thank you that you joyfully gave us your Son and that you delight in giving us every good thing. God, I ask now for a greater measure of your Holy Spirit in my life. I want to look more like Jesus, and I want to pray spirit to Spirit. Please give me the ability to pray in tongues. Thank you that you hear me and that your answer is already yes and amen. I receive the grace to pray in tongues now, in Jesus' name.

ABOUT THE AUTHOR

•   •   •

Rebecca Ribnick is an adventure-loving author and pastor. She's passionate about living a joyful life dependent on God's faithfulness and seeing how much of heaven she can contain inside of her. While Rebecca used to find speaking in tongues super strange, God has changed her heart on that topic and many others. (However, her love for baked goods remains the same.)

In addition to speaking in tongues, Rebecca is also passionate about healing. Her own story includes an unexpected and radical healing that literally changed the course of her life and led her to places she never thought she'd go—like the witch doctor's house. For more of that story and many others, as well as a deep dive into what the Bible says about healing, check out her book *HOPE: A Practical Guide to Praying for Healing,* which is available on Amazon or through your local bookstore. Visit rebeccaribnick.com for more information.

Made in the USA
Coppell, TX
03 January 2023